360 Life Skills For All!

C P Bansal

BlueRose ONE.com
Stories Matter
NewDelhi • London

BLUEROSE PUBLISHERS
India | U.K.

For permissions requests or inquiries regarding this publication, please contact:

BLUEROSE PUBLISHERS
www.BlueRoseONE.com
info@bluerosepublishers.com
+91 8882 898 898
+4407342408967

ISBN: 978-93-7139-843-5

Cover Design: Aman Sharma
Typesetting: Pooja Sharma

First Edition: September 2025

LIFE SKILL S

PREFACE

A single idea can change very much, for the better in our life. Many a time we are in a conflict what to do & what not to do. 360 Life Skills in the book are an attempt in this direction. If followed in right earnest, hopefully every life skill can guide us to act prudently & pragmatically. Life Skills cover a wide range like love, relations, God, inspiration, nature, education, sports, health, careers & many others. Language has been deliberately kept simple so that all can comprehend easily & benefit.

First I am grateful to God, who enabled me to write & get the book published. My thoughts go to my father in heaven, who always attempted to give me knowledge in many fields. I am grateful to all, who inspired me to write this book. I have gratitude specially for my friends Teri Headrick, Maria Alejandra, Dee Marlow of USA and Hannelore Heidenreich of Germany: who always inspired me to write creative & useful for all mankind!

LIFE. SKILL 1 TO FALL IN LOVE

Maybe true for worldly or false love! In real. Sublime love we rise in love!

LIFE SKILL 2.

Show love, respect to all, even strangers! Among them there can be Angels!

LIFE SKILL 3

When you get new friend, don't neglect old friends! Each friend deserves due love, respect!

LIFE SKILL 4

Don't break thread of love or friendship with jerk!

Each relationship needs patience & selflessness!

LIFE SKILL 5

Show light to one in dark! This will illuminate you as well! Love to loveless: You will get magnified love!

LIFE SKILL 6

Happiness, Knowledge, Love, Light, Peace multiply by sharing! So share lavishly!

LIFE SKILL 7

Don't fear tough times! Darker the night, brighter the dawn! Nothing can prevent glittering dawn!

LIFE SKILL 8

Any person or situation can be inspiration! Can guide to proper path & destination!

LIFE SKILL 9

Propagate Love, Light, Peace, Joyl They interconnect and connect all mankind!

LIFE SKILL 10 HATE MAY DEFEAT LOVE FOR A WHILE. DARK MAY BLOCK LIGHT TEMPORARILY!

Nothing can block

Love, Light permanently! So propagate or be

Love, Light!

LIFE SKILL 11 DUSK CAN BE AS

beautiful as dawn. So don't relent, be inactive at twilight, of life! -

LIFE SKILL 12

Love everyone whom you meet in life's journey! If fail, be indifferent. But hate none, as hate devastates self

LIFE SKILL 13

God & devil both are inside us. We have to deactivate devil & catalyse connect with inner God!

LIFE SKILL 14

On a righteous path don't aspire others to follow! Go solo! A long line is sure to emulate & follow!

LIFE SKILL 15

Life is short, rejoice each-day! Illuminate with love, light, hope & faith: Each Day!

LIFE SKILL 16

Count your blessings, not problems. Be grateful for them, You are sure to be blessed more!

LIFE SKILL 17

Beauty of heart, soul illuminates inside. This transmutes to facial beauty & glow!

LIFE SKILL 18

Personality largely depends on heredity & environment. Heredity is fixed, so give best possible environment to yourself & children!

LIFE SKILL 19

Follow Gratitude. It creates fortitude, to tackle life's vicissitudes!

LIFE. SKILL. 20

Love your nation but rise above nation. Love world, de facto a big family!

LIFE SKILL 21

Love your religion. This is the best! But respect all religions! All have much in common!

LIFE SKILL 22

Lack of faith destroys each relation from human to Divine! Have faith in no dearth!

LIFE SKILL 23

Avoid doubts, that destroy love, friendship or ay relation!

LIFE SKILL 24

Present is Most important: shapes future, live in it & make the most! Past too is important: for lessons & cherishing merry moments!

LIFE SKILL 25

Look above for inspiration. Look behind for lessons & rectification. Look ahead for destination!

LIFE SKIL 26

Life is a continuous journey Halt for rest &'rejuvenating : but don't stop before ultimate destination!

LIFE SKILL 27

Home is Best! Joy is not in Paris or Rome! It's in a beautiful home! It's not in beautiful marbles or furniture! It's in mutual love & nurture! -

LIFE LESSON 28

Value One! God One! Religion (Truth) Just One! Nature One! Humanity One! World, a big family, One!

LIFE. LESSON 29

Value Seven! Continents seven! Colors of rainbow seven! Week days seven! Musical notes Seven! Major seas Seven!

LIFE SKILL 30

Way to Heavenly Father, Mother initiates from father & mother! Their service is a lead to God!

LIFE SKILL 31

Love all mankind! At all costs be kind! In kindness, never lag behind!

LIFE SKILL 32

Go with nature, It's easy & prudent. Going against nature is swimming upstream.

LIFE SKILL 33

Practice generosity, charity, humanity sans formality! Show off diminishes their magnanimity!

LIFE SKILL 34

Radiate light like Radium! Propagate love like Saints! Propagate peace as Messengers of God! Love, Light, Peace are dire needs!

LIFE SKILL 35

Never demand from God! Heavenly Father knows our needs! Even a good father knows sans telling!

LIFE SKILL 36

Mind is one, focus on either God or worldly! Only Love or God is imperishable!

LIFE SKILL 37

Practise: Best victory: Victory over self Best possession: Heavenly Bank Balance of benign deeds(Karma)!

LIFE SKILL 38

Focus on quality of life! Swami Vivekanand, Ramtirath John Keats didn't touch 40: But became immortal!

LIFE SKILL 39

If wrong, don't delay effective & prompt apology! Apology after damage is useless!.

LIFE SKILL 40

Forgiveness is virtue in almost all religions! Forgive & Forget before forgiving: Otherwise a sad feeling persists!

LIFE SKILL 41

Cut aggression by compassion! Make compassion a passion, rather obsession!

LIFE SKILL 42

Seek good in each situation. Any situation can be inspiration. And just fail frustration!

LIFE SKILL 43

Don't be selfish & self centred ! But self is good in self-realization, self-elevation & self-assessment!

LIFE. SKILL 44

Challenge Handicap! It is only in mind! Severely challenged: Helen Keller, Stephen Hawking& Archer Sheetal Devi have achieved what, even capable are only dreaming!

LIFE. SKILL 45

Be in movement, upward or towards the set goal. Meaningful life means movement!

LIFE SKILL 46

It's important: When to speak! What-to speak! How to speak! And not to speak, when necessary!

LIFE. SKILL 47

Wish, pray good for all others. In fact there are no others. Whatever we wish & pray affects us too!

LIFE SKILL 48

Practise love in every manifestation. Mother or father's love is matchless. All love their children. Be a parent for the loveless!

LIFE SKILL 49

Physical work doesn't tire much! • Worrying, stress, bring real exertion & fatigue!

LIFE SKILL 50

Eradicate hate & propagate love! Love creates, recreates & invigorates! Hate only devastates!

LIFE SKILL 51

Each vice in us is virus! Ego alone germinates arrogance, insensitivity & lack of empathy. Give a go to ego!

LIFE SKILL 52

Live love, light, peace, everyday! Receive all three magnified everyday!

LIFE SKILL 53

There is crowd of people! Good people you meet are roses among thorns! Make & preserve relationship with them!

LIFE SKILL 54

In any relationship, for peace: When one shows anger, other to keep mum! Clarify your view only when heat cools down!

LIFE SKILL 55

All say follow your heart! Heart is mad, can mislead! Using both heart & mind is more prudent!

LIFE SKILL 56

Go with the eternal, not ephemeral! Only Truth, Love & God are eternal I Dant fluctuate, don't terminate!

LIFE SKILL 57

Consider your intuition. Intuition is calling of soul! More sacred the soul, more correct the intuition!

LIFE SKILL 58

For abundant problems, seek the best solution: Love! Sadly true love is most deficient!

LIFE SKILL 59

Cast a glance on those in dark! For them be a spark! History there's who eradicate dark!

LIFE SKILL 60

If advertently or inadvertently done any wrong, don't regret. Regret is retrograde Needful is rectification & amendment.

LIFE SKILL 61

Always plan day's work in morning. Start doing resolutely priority wise. Assess at the end of day. The remaining start from next morning, without frustration.

LIFE SKILL 62

Work with positive mindset, with smiles. Better output, less exertion.

LIFE SKILL 63

Never trust a man who talks bad about others. He will talk bad about you in your absence.

LIFE SKILL 64

Chose wisely your goal. Work resolutely with positive mindset & eyes set on goal.

LIFE SKILL 65

Happiness is inner. No harm in seeking outer, in nature or any where! There's no upper limit in happiness.

LIFE LESSON 66

Truth, virtues ever last! Lies, vices are transient! One can live longest in love, but not in hate!

LIFE SKILL 67

Autumn is no less Beautiful than Spring! Same way each stage of life has particular importance! Live with enthusiasm ,your stage of Life

LIFE SKILL 68

Fear is our worst enemy! Eradicate fear, attempt & attain cherished goal!

LIFE SKILL 69

Don't fret at adversity. Fools, Cowards fret at - adversity. Wise, Brave transmute this to opportunity!

LIFE SKILL 70

If hurt anyone, effective apology is necessary. It ought to be from heart in suave words, repeated till offended gets cool.

Apology must not be followed by argument.

LIFE SKILL 71

We are temporary tenants on earth! Real owners are our progeny! Consider as your main duty to leave better planet for them!

LIFE LESSON 72

Set the goal & path! Love the path & proceed relentlessly! You are at destination!

LESSON 73

Find faults in self & amend! Seek good in others & commend!

LIFE SKILL 74

Pursue love in Every

way! Each relation, friendship, hobbies all are manifestations of love!

LIFE SKILL 75

Practise love from fundamental to transcendental! Sublime love isn't easy, it's climbing steep rock!

LIFE SKILL 76

Seek Knowledge, logic both. Knowledge is power! Logic is greater power! Wisdom, largely inherent is superpower!

LIFE SKILL 77

Don't fear storm. Storm is transient, calm ever lasts! In fact, storm is preceded & followed boy calm!

LIFE SKILL 78

Life is journey! In journey we often meet people, as we are! So, we ought to be good!

LIFE SKILL 79

All world one No fences, no walls, no barriers! Only bridges!

LIFE SKILL 80

Rise high but like tall trees with firm roots! Like tall tower s with deep foundation! And not like a kite.

LIFE SKILL 81

Life is wave with crests & troughs! Accept ups & downs stoically, happily!

LIFE SKILL 82

Practise Love, a vital life -force! Sans love, we cease to be human. We are merely a robot!

LIFE SKILL 83

Don't degrade by being selfish & self centred. But self is important too, in self-amendment, assessment & realisation!

LIFE SKILL 84

Practise austerity, humanity, honesty, generosity & sanctity! Life becomes sheer beauty & dignity!

LIFE SKILL 85

When weary of considerations, exertion: Seek refuge in-nature! Nature does replenish & nurture!

LIFE SKILL 86

Introspect by: Who am I? What for I am! What is my immediate destination? It's the way for self-exaltation!

LIFE SKILL 87

Avoid pollution. Outer pollution is harmful. Inner pollution by ego, greed, hate is worst!

LIFE SKILL 88

Through thick and thin, hold hand of a friend, don't desert. It's way to assert sincerity in friendship.

LIFE SKILL 89

Have faith. Faith in self and faith in God are the two wheels of our vehicle! Only they keep us going & don't let us fail!

LIFE. SKILL.90

Have positive outlook. For one with positive outlook, this very world is Heavenl For a cynic is hell.

LIFE SKILL 91

Initiate each virtue from self! Love, the greatest virtue, too, must start from self & propagate fast!

LIFE. SKILL.92

Love & laugh lavishly! -All inclusive love & laughter are wholesome. They heal us holistically.

LIFE SKILL 93

There are many attributes to beauty! A few are: Pleasing behavior, benevolence & infectious smile.

LIFE SKILL 94

Don't overburden by every responsibility. Leave some to destiny & Almighty. Time itself eventually solves many problems.

LIFE SKILL 95

Move to light. Darkness doesn't go by crying dark, dark! Light a little lamp & dark goes stark!

LIFE SKILL 96

Terminate hate, greed & lust! From dust we merged, in dust will merge. Be Kind and give life a positive thrust.

LIFE SKILL 97

Start from Self: Self-love, discipline & realization! End from self: Ego & selfishness! Practise austerity generosity & charity!

LIFE SKILL 98

Let compassion become a passion, rather obsession! Compassion has countless splendid repercussions!

LIFE SKILL 99

Be kind to be beloved of people & Providence. All virtues merge in kindness. It sheds inner & outer darkness!

LIFE.SKILL 100

Feel power of one! Paths many, goal one! Messangers many, Message one! Rivers many, Sea one! Tenants many, planet one! We're one!!

LIFE LESSON 101

Learn from lotus to rise & shine in mud, and to enhance elegance of world!

LIFE, SKILL. 102

Avoid greed! God meets not desires, but our needs! There is no end to greed! Eradicate greed, minimise needs!

LIFE SKILL 103

Let no barrier come in way of friendship & love! Distance matters, but must not deter!

LIFE SKILL 104

Don't be tempted for more land on earth! Capture space in Heaven by Virtues, Love & Kindness, in no dearth! -

LIFE. SKILL.105

Generosity borings happiness! Do generosity, charity with no expectations! Expectations can cause frustration

LIFE, KILL .106

All shed tears! Shed tears alone or before God! These are purgatory! Share only with confidante or God your story!

Others can make mockery!

LIFE SKILL 107

On a righteous path don't delay for company! Go solo, now! A long line is sure to emulate & follow you!

LIFE SKILL 108

Follow gratitude. Gratitude betters attitude! Positive attitude adds to fortitude, so essential to tackle life's viciccitudes!

LIFE SKILL 109

Life is a flowing river! Flow with the. flow, downstream! Be natural & practical!

LIFE SKILL 110

Life is too short to love! Don't waste in animosity, ego & hate

LIFE SKILL 111

Never mind if words fail: Silence speaks. Expressions speak. Music speaks!

LIFE SKILL 112

Love the path, however tough! if there's no path, make one! Let path & destination, both be inspiration!

LIFE SKILL 113

Start the day with positive affirmation & prayer! End day with self-assessment & prayer! Then hopefully, no despair!

LIFE SKILL 114

Be humane & humble. Do charity with generosity. Specially for ones in adversity & suffering humanity! Do with no Formality!

LIFE SKILL 115

Give before receiving! Forget before forgiving! Behave as you expect behaving!

LIFE SKILL 116

Follow earnestly Sayings: Excess of everything is bad! Middle Path of Buddha! Extremes are never: good! These are essentially same!

LIFE SKILL 117

Over exploitation results in retaliation! Same with kind nature, which gets furious on over exploitation!!

LIFE SKILL 118

Be a rose, that flourishes in as hostile surroundings as thorns!

LIFE SKILL 119

Chose Love! Love is light. Hate is dark. Dark can't conquer light. Hate can't defeat love!

LIFE SKILL 120

Chose Love. Love is light. Hare is dark. Dark can't conquer light. Hate can't defeat love!

LIFE SKILL 121

If your plan fails, don't despair! Divine plan is acting for you, far superior to yours!

LIFE SKILL .122

Accept all relations as they are! Amending self is easier & wiser!!

LIFE SKILL 123

Don't impose your wish on your child. Search his interest & aptitude! Encourage & inspire in that direction!

LIFE SKILL 124

None can help all! If in a day, we help one, inspire one & cheer up one: Day is Successful!

LIFE SKILL 125

Correct a wise politely, he will accept, appreciate & thank you! Avoid correcting a foolish, he won't accept, rather can hate you!

LIFE SKILL 126

Soul & Supreme Soul, both are inside us! Yet very few can connect them! Those we Connect, get enlightenment, like Buddha, Guru Nanak!

LIFE SKILL 127

Conquer: Dark with light! 0 Hate with love. Vicewith virtue. And enmity with friendship!

LIFE SKILL 128

All shed tears. Shed tears alone or before God. These are purgatory. Share only with Confidante or God your story.

LIFE SKILL 129

Have a sacred soul. Intuition is calling of soul. More sacred the soul, more Correct the intuition.

LIFE SKILL 130

Treat all world as one big family. No differences, no offenses, no fences & no barriers. Only bridges.

LIFE SKILL 131

Take major decisions as marriage after major thinking: positive, negative aspects both. Major decisions have long time repercussions.

LIFE SKILL 132

If you aspire for a top career as civil services, doctor etc, hope for the best, do your best. But be prepared for the worst. Have a plan B too, as competition is really cut throat.

LIFE SKILL 133

Practise good etiquettes. They cost nothing, yet please all & pay back with heavy dividends.

LIFE S KILL 134

Do kindness, benevolence, cooperation sans expectation! Expectations generally lead to frustrations!

LIFE SKILL 135

Al returns, so, wish & act good, All will return with dividends!

LIFE SKILL 136

Life is movement. Move from: Dark to light! Orthodox to scientific! Parsimonious to Magnanimous!

LIFE SKILL 137

Do interior decoration of home by love, respect, laughter & peace Decoration is less by paints & furniture!

LIFE SKILL 138

Love All inclusive! All world a big family! LIFE also means: Love Is For Everyone!

LIFE SKILL 139

Don't break thread of love with jerk! It takes long time & pains to build palace of love: Breaking can be in seconds!

LIFE SKILL 140

Let go & cherish. All grief & melancholy must eventually perish! Surrender to god & relish!

LIFE SKILL 141

Beautify present time!

Time fleets but memories remain. Present actions make future memories.

LIFE SKILL 142

Don't relent at twilight of life. Needful is, more the age, more care & less stress!

LIFE SKILL 143

Sacrifice all for peace, soul and Supreme Soul! No sacrifice is too big for these!

LIFE. SKILL.144

Don't be a fool to fret at adversity! Be wise to transmute adversity to opportunity!

LIFE SKILL 145

Propagate own light as stars. or transmit light of greats as moon! But do illuminate with light! Inner light is generally deficient!

LIFE, SKILL.146

Speak, but think before speaking: 1 What to speak. 2.When to speak 3, How to speak! Speaking should b suave & soothing!

LIFE. SKILL.147

Start from Self: Self-love, discipline & realization! End from self: Ego & selfishness! Practise austerity & generosity!

LIFE. SKILL. 148

Transcend from: Conservative to liberal! Orthodox to scientific! National to whole world! And frugal to generous!

LIFE SKILL 149

In Hinduism Earth is rightly called Mother Earth! Care & serve her as mother, a living organism! It's the best way to save deteriorating environment!

LIFE SKILL 150

Practise philanthropy, humanity, humility & austerity! These surely endear us to Almighty!

LIFE SKILL 151

Elevate with positive attitude, perception & qualities! Don't diminish with negative traits!

LIFE SKILL 152

Propagate peace! For peace, no price is too great. Sans, peace none can progress & elevate!

LIFE SKILL 153

Keep your inner child active & awake till very last! It's a way to purposeful & healthy longevity!!

LIFE SKILL 154

Use kind, soothing words. Words can assault or assuage! Chose wisely!

LIFE SKILL 155

Life is movement: Move with fellow travelers joyfully! Life is game: Play in sportsman spirit!

LIFE SKILL 156

Compete with others in your field: Healthy Competition elevates. Compete with self to become your better version!

LIFE SKILL 157

Transmute 'adversities to opportunities! Cowards fret & fume at adversities!

Braves turn to opportunities!

LIFE SKILL 158

Multiply joy, kindness knowledge de facto each virtue by sharing!

LIFE SKILL 159

Even if we assume charms, spells effect: They get ineffective it we have a protective shield of God's love & grace!

LIFE SKILL 160

At twilight of life, don't relent! Dusk is no less beautiful than dawn! With motivation, move on!

LIFE SKILL 161

Know something of everything & everything of something! Knowledge is as vast as Univer se!

LIFE SKILL 162

Life's essence: Patience, Tolerance, Acceptance , Magnificence & Benevolence! Pursue with perseverance!

LIFE SKILL 163

Say now, no to hate, apathy, anger & ego. For a meaningful life, give them a permanent go!

LIFE SKILL 164

Life is a game, play it Wisely, gladly & relentlessly! If win, celebrate! If lose, accept stoically & restart with renewed zeal to win!

LIFE SKILL 165

Life is a journey! We can't stop, we can only haul in between for rejuvenating! Walk till destination! After destination move for a higher destination!

LIFE, SKILL 166

Focus more on inner beauty, that results from inner glow caused by truth, honesty, integrity & kindness!

LIFE SKILL 167

One lamp lights innumerable lamps. Likewise, three: Love, Kindness & truth activate all virtues in us. Lead on path from human to Divine!

LIFE SKILL 168

Kindness Benevolence, Forgiveness, Patience Acceptance are lead to Providence!!

LIFE SKILL 169

Remain in movement! Life means movement. Earth, sun, milky way, galaxies, de facto whole universe is in movement Stagnant is detriment.

LIFE SKILL 170

Cast a glance for those in dark. For them be a spark! History their's who shed dark & thus make mark!

LIFE SKILL 171

Be Generous always, generous are happy always! Generosity acts bothways!

LIFE SKILL 172

Share generosity, Love, peace, joy, knowledge. They follow strange law: They multiply by sharing!

LIFE SKILL 173

Serve elders, Guru & Saints! Seek their blessings! These will help you in most dire need & critical times!

LIFE SKILL 174

Practise some art! Art in any form, as music, is outlet of emotions & a thing of beauty to cheer forever!

LIFE SKILL 175

Atom has inore power - than obvious! You have more dormant capability & potential than you know! Just activate dormant & elevate!

LIFE SKILL 176

Continue communication! Just as plant dies without nurture, love or any relation dies without communication, love & care!

LIFE SKILL 177

Win heart of your enemy. It's tough, but feasible. Real victory is not defeating or killing: It's winning heart!

LIFE SKILL 178

Don't tell about your qualities, these will reveal naturally. Blossom doesn't boast of its beauty! Diamond doesn't tell it's worth!

LIFE SKILL 179

No destination is too difficult to end in frustration! We must walk in inspiration! Idlers get nowhere! For success we need action & dare!

LIFE SKILL 180

In the well-being of all lies ours'! Our actions, wishes return to us magnified! So, wish & act finest to be dignified.

LIFE SKILL 181

Suppressed emotions can tear inside! So, cry alone, share with God or confidante your story! Others can make a mockery!

LIFE SKILL 182

Conquer negativity with positive thoughts & actions. Light conquers dark! Gods conquer devils! Virtue conquers vice! Love conquers hate!

LIFE SKILL 183

Don't use A.I, photos! Don't use cosmetics in excess! Who loves or likes you, will do so in your natural self!

LIFE SKILL 184

If you are burdened by too many works, prioritize & do one at a time with concentration! Then all success, no frustration!

LIFE SKILL 185

Have no frustration at failure! Failure also means: Falling Again In Love with Unending Resolve Endlessly!

LIFE SKILL 186

No work is small, Love your work! Work with smiles & dedication! Then no frustration, no exertion!

LIFE SILL 187

For- splendid success, have a wise thought, then planned action relentlessly! If succeed good! If failure, no frustration, rectification to renewed efforts relentlessly. Success is assured!

LIFE SKILL 188

Tough paths often lead to beautiful: destinations! Love both path & destination. Move ahead with no

procrastination!

LIFE SKILL 189

Many sad events happen unnoticed! Take ignorance as a bliss! Forgetting sad, bad past too is a bliss!

LIFESKILL 190

Focus on positivity, beauty & not on ugly & negativity. This very world would seem beautiful Eden Garden!

LIFE SKILL 191

Transmute Love, Life from static to dynamic! This way love, life will become vibrant!

LIFE SKILL 192

Happiness, Sadness both are infectious! Spread infection of Happiness! Redress Sadness yourself or sharing with confidante!

LIFE SKILL 193

Enhance healthy longevity with: Generosity, magnanimity, adaptability, sanctity, austerity & flexibility in all practicality!

LIFE SKILL 194

Failure is stepping stone to success! Follow Golden rule:

Hope for the best, be prepared for the worst! Then no

frustration or depression!

LIFE SKILL 195

By opening up, buds become beautiful blossoms! Open heart with loved ones! Then need won't arise to cut with scissors!

LIFE SKILL 196

Sow seeds of love, kindness, generosity & humanity! Reap bounty of these & get God's Blessings in plenty!

LIFE SKILL 197

Gain or loss is law of nature Move with nature! Bear loss however big, strongly stoically!

LIFE SKILL 198

Use kind, suave words to assuage, not to assault! Words constitute sermons, hymns, blessings & mantras.

Very words can be threats abuses & curses!

LIFE SKILL 199

Real fight is within, between virtue & vice. Real victory is over self. Conquer self by controlling self & desires!

LIFE SKILL 200

Fortune is a wave with crests and troughs! Enjoy ride on both, with equanimity and fortitude!

LIFE SKILL 201

According to situation: Silence, eloquence both are important! In row, be reticent. To express feelings or to comfort: be eloquent!

LIFE SKILL 202

Accept the situation. Trust, Divine plan is better than ours'! What seems bad now, can prove Blessing in disguise later!

LIFE SKILL 203

Adjustment, Acceptance Patience lead to better relations! Inculcate all these by following Middle Path of Buddha!

LIFE SKILL 204

Love your nation, Yet rise above nation! Exalt self by practising: All world is a big family!

LIFE SKILL 205

count your innumerable blessings with optimism. Even Walking is a blessing: There are many confined to wheel chair. Be grateful for all similar Blessings!

LIFE SKILL 206

TRUE PILGRIMAGE: *For son, daughter: Service of parents! For daughter in law: Service of in laws!*

LIFE SKILL 207

Consider: Home is Best Joy is not in Paris or Rome! It's in a beautiful home! It's not in beautiful marbles or furniture! It's in mutual love & nurture!

LIFE SKILL 208

Knowledge, Logic & Wisdom are important. Knowledge is power. Blend of Knowledge logic & wisdom is super power.

LIFE SKILL 209

Gratitude, Positive & scientific attitude are essential to tackle life's vicissitudes! Practise with fortitude!

LIFE SKILL 210

Forget before forgiving & cherish. Each grief will eventually perish. Live with zest, not merely exist!

LIFE SKILL 211

Let go pride, arrogance;& ego! Many flaws will forever go.

LIFE SKILL 212

Happiness is generally occasional! Make it perennial: In compassion, contentment, be perpetual!

LIFE SKILL 213

If at all a rift comes in any relation: Be the first to cement the gap. Delay can make gap wider: Even irreparable!

LIFE SKILL 214

Never belittle little! Little words make quotes & sermons. Bricks make palaces: Little cells make big animals & trees. Tiny atoms make all matter, even universe!

LIFE SKILL 215

Grip of virtues is loose; Grip of vices very firm. Hold virtues tightly & release vices promptly!

LIFE SKILL 216

Present is most important, shapes future, live in it & make the most! Past too is important: for lessons & cherishing merry moments.

LIFE SKILL 217

Look above for inspiration. Look behind for lessons & rectification. Look ahead for destination!

LIFE SKILL 218

Relations are like beautiful crockery, Brittle! Can't afford neglect, even little! Need communication & nurture to sparkle!

LIFE SKILL 219

Human life is rare gift from God & one! Live it to the fullest, with full positivity!

LIFE SKILL 220

Show generosity by giving company to someone suffering from loneliness! This is a trouble in itself & leads to many troubles!

LIFE SKILL 221

Treasure your real friends & relations. Many a person with 5000 Facebook friends don't attract even 5 at demise!!

LIFE SKILL 222

Avoid smartphone excessive use! Smartphone addiction is relatively new, but already caught millions globally! Thei r physical, mental health is badly impaired!!

LIFE SKILL 223

Avoid frustration, tension, stress, anxiety etc. These can lead to depression, a stubborn disease. Remain busy creatively, joyfully to avoid all these!

LIFE SKILL 224

Fill life with peace, hope, faith, kindness & prosperity. Intellectual prosperity is superior & durable to material prosperity!!

LIFE SKILL 225

Help someone even fully knowing he can't help you back! Such help will come to you in unexpected way, from unexpected source!!

LIFE SKILL 226

Don't get upset when someone rejects you! He is failing to know your real worth! Only a jeweller knows worth of diamond!

LIFE SKILL 227

For upkeep of healthy durable relationship: No lies! No cheating. And no false promises!!

LIFE SKILL 228

Kindness is religion & a great virtue! But don't be kind to ungrateful people! They can misuse or abuse your kindness!!

LIFE SKILL 229

Seek material prosperity, but with honesty & austerity. Once you achieve this, share a part of this with deprived & really needy!

LIFE SKILL 230

Material prosperity is not bad. But strive for better intellectual & spiritual prosperity! They pave way for overall excellence

LIFE SKILL 231

Accept challenges & act resolutely. You will see you are more able & capable than you know! Challenges bring out the very FINEST in you, even dormant qualities

LIFE SKILL 232

Be tolerant. Don't walk away from any genuine relation for a few flaws! No one is perfect, without any flaw!!

LIFE SKILL 233

Accept people, friends & relations as they are! For, we can't change anyone much! Only-we can adapt ourselves!

LIFE SKILL 234

From tiniest electron to several light years huge galaxies, all are in continuous motion! We too ought to emulate & remain in movement!

LIFE SKILL 235

Remain in the world, but don't get over attached. Over attachment makes sadi Be as boat, that remains in water, yet above it!

LIFE SKILL 236

For upkeep of good memory, mental & physical health keep your inner child active & awake! Adopt child's inherent love & honesty!

LIFE SKILL 237

GRATITUDE: Inculcate Gratitude as an attitude. It enhances positive attitude & fortitude, so essential to tackle life's vicissitudes!

LIFE SKILL 238

With hate, anger & ego we only exist & somehow survive! Don't just exist, with love, peace, humanity & humility, rise & thrive!

LIFE SKILL 239

Never demand from God! Even a good father knows his son's needs! Heavenly Father is the wisest & surely knows! Just be grateful& have more and more!

LIFE SKILL 240

Don't grieve: If money lost, earn again! If lost a relation, keep him alive by following his footprints! If health, recuperate with zeal!

LIFE- SKILL 241

Affinity for world can result in infinity from God! Have Affinity for God, it will bless you with His affection!

LIFE SKILL 242

What tension is! It's the void between achievement & aspiration! Bridge the void & evolve successful, jubilant sans tension!

LIFE SKILL 243

Love from heart & soul! Never hurt a loving heart! It will leave for you a big hole!

LIFE SKILL 244

Focus more on inner beauty, that results from inner glow caused by truth, honesty, integrity & kindness!

LIFE SKILL 245

Serve parents, offer blossoms now! Useless after demise! Way to Heavenly Father, Mother starts from parents!

LIFE SKILL 246

Be Calm at any cost. Calm is mightier than storm! Storm is preceded & followed by calm!

LIFE SKILL 247

Seek good in every person & situation. They can be inspiration. Just fail frustration!

LIFE SKILL 248

Make your home happy, heaven & shrine! It's feasible by mutual love, regards, patience & infectious smiles!

LIFE SKILL 249

Love now! Love is basic need as food, clothing & shelter! But Love true: Don't degrade to lust, selfishness & infatuation!

LIFE SKILL 250

Essence of life is coexistence! Earth belongs to all. Live & let live: With patience, balance & benevolence!

LIFE SKILL 251

Despite degradation of values, there's no dearth of Angels disguised as humans on earth! Recognize & revere them in no dearth!

LIFE SKILL 252

Love & Birds know no barriers, visa etc. They move freely. Let your love flow freely to all meeting you in journey called life!

LIFE SKILL 253

Love needs no language, Love can speak in silence! But many a time love needs eloquence!

LIFE SKILL 254

Happiness is a matter of priority! In: descending order: Time management. Adjustment, Relation, Generosity,

Positivity & last of all Money for needs!

LIFE SKILL 255

Love both perishables & imperishable God & Nature! When love with perishables will perish love with imperishables will support & sustain!

LIFE SKILL 256

Way to Happiness & Beauty:

Benevolence, Balance, Patience, Tolerance & Acceptance all enhance our happiness & beauty! Surprisingly all are free!

LIFE SKILL 257

Divine Light, love, peace are essence of our existence. Inner darkness is more damaging than outer darkness. Practise, propagate, in abundance: Love, light & peace!

LIFE SKILL 258

Dont belittle little creatures! They are beauties in miniature! Lily, firefly, butterfly live transient! Yet, they are pretty & vibrant!

LIFE SKILL 259

Law of Reflection & Newtons law of equal & opposite reaction: Hold good to human life! What we wish, think or act returns to us, often magnified!

LIFE SKILL 260

May be dormant, you have substantial potential. Elevate from fundamental to transcendental. Remember no accomplishment is accidental!

LIFE SKILL 261

One good turn deserves another. If one extends hand, hold his hand warmly & promptly!

LIFE SKILL 262

Like pure, impure blood each person has good, bad traits. Accordingly we think, act good or bad. Prudence lies in activating goodness & deactivating bad traits!

LIFE SKILL 263

Elevate from dark to light: Superstitious to scientific: Ignorant to learned: Fanatic to flexible & vicious to virtuous!

LIFE SKILL 264

Each educated teach one: There's no dearth of education! Each affluent help one: Poverty eradication! Each one feed at least one: This very world becomes Heaven!

LIFE SKILL 265

Heaven or hell are no geographic location! They are in mind's condition! Every place is heaven with positive attitude & perception!

LIFE SKILL 266

Way to healthy, happy life: Contentment! To be benevolent, tolerant & with age not to relent! And upkeep interests!

LIFE SKILL 267

Don't over burden by every responsibility! Leave some to time, destiny & Almighty! Time itself, eventually solves many problems!

LIFE SKILL 268

Start from Self: Self love, discipline & realization! End from self: Ego & selfishness! Practise austerity & generosity!

LIFE SKILL 269

Love, kindness, empathy, care or compassion: Whatever you give to others, you receive with dividends!

LIFE SKILL 270

It's a folly to stoop to revenge! Offender is devastated by his own offence! Be forgiving to receive God's blessings!

LIFE SKILL 271

SUCCESS *also* Means: *Successive, Unending, Consistent, Continuous Efforts to Surely Succeed!*

LIFE SKILL 272

People who uplift, inspire you are your best friends! Not only cherish their company, rather treasure them!

LIFE SKILL 273

Consider debt as a disease. As far as possible avoid debt and purchase on EMI's!!

LIFE SKILL 274

Never lose hope & faith. Specially in illness. With hope & faith illness is cured comparatively fast!

LIFE SKILL 275

Will power is as powerful as knowledge! Both help to reach goal, specially in tough conditions

LIFE. SKILL 276

More a learned, wise knows, more he knows what he doesn't know! Discussion with such a person is always uplifting!

LIFE SKILL 277

A fool thinks he knows everything & needs no advice So, don't waste time, energy on advising or discussion with a fool!

LIFE SKILL 278

For inner Joy, minimize needs, maximise adjustment & contentment! And end greed!

LIFE SKILL 279

Look with optimist outlook, there is no dearth of blessings for you. Be grateful for more blessings!

LIFE. SKILL 280

Virtues have lose grip. Vices have Strong grip! Turn it around! Let virtues have strong grip!

LIFE SKILL 281

Have heart of a little kid! It's purest & has love & light! Activate your inner child to exalt!

LIFE SKILL 282

All reality in life causes monotony! Add some fantasy, this adds spice to life!

LIFE SKILL 283

Be contented, grateful for whatever you have! You will find more pleasures, blessings coming your way!

LIFE, SKILL. 284

Love humanity & Almighty abundantly! Only love for humanity & Almighty will accompany us when we depart!

LIFE SKILL 285

Sincere apology & forgiveness: Both are Divine virtues! Don't delay at all: Delay loses impact!

LIFE SKILL 286

Way to success: Recognize your aptitude & capability. Set path & goal. Plan prudently. Act resolutely & relentlessly. Success is assured!

LIFE. SKILL 287

God is within! Going shrines too is important: For focus & relishing beauty of temples. Also, beauty of nature around many among them.

LIFE SKILL 288

Love your profession, work with smiles! If you find it impossible, then better change profession!

LIFE SKILL 289

-Find faults in self & amend! Find good

in others &

commend! This makes you your better version & popular among all you come across.

LIFE SKILL 290

When weary of realities of life, tour to nature! But don't

escape: Escape further adds to problems!

LIFE. SKILL. 291

Seek beauty, it is everywhere!

Specially in God's own manifestation, Naturel

LIFE SKILL 292

Love itself is

imperishable. Love is imperishable as God, Nature more

than anyone, anything else.

LIFE SKILL 293

Follow footprints of greats. Create emutable footprints & leave for others to follow!

LIFE LESSON 294

Have less desires for more happiness! And who have no desires, are emperor of emperors!

LIFE SKILL 295

Plants love & grow in light! Humans too love & need light! So reflect or radiate your own light!

LIFE SKILL 296

Be great by great deeds. Greater by love & peace. Far greater by all inclusive and Divine love

LIFE SKILL 297

Pursue friendship or love, that know no barrier. Distance of course matters, but can't deter!

LIFE SKILL 298

Minimize needs. Eliminate greeds, they are limitless! They will destroy happiness!

LIFE SKILL 299

Have gratitude, the best attitude! It creates positive attitude & fortitude to tackle life's vicissitudes!

LIFE SKILL 300

Have happiness, that lies in contentment, adjustment, no resentment & behaving pleasant.

LIFE SKILL 301

Retain merry moments! Sad past let go and cherish! With time all grief, pain must perish!

LIFE SKILL 302

Be self dependent. Avoid expectations. These often lead to frustrations!

LIFE SKILL 303

Be constructive, not destructive. Construction takes long time, destruction can be very soon, in seconds only. This is true for both: material structures & relations!

LIFE SKILL 304

Avoid consulting astrologer. Our destinies are written at the time of our birth. Flow downstream, with the flow of life.

LIFE SKILL 305

Advise or teach anyone by example once or twice. If one is willing to accept, will accept. Otherwise, won't accept at any rate.

LIFE SKILL 306

If you are a teacher, inspire students to have passion for knowledge. Giving examples of life & learning of great men is very helpful.

LIFE SKILL 307

Be a rose, that flourishes in tough conditions as thorns! In favorable condition, generally anyone can flourish.

LIFE SKILL 308

Learn from anyone, anything. From rivers, movement. From trees, giving shelter & fruit, even to stone pelters. From birds, soaring high .

LIFE SKILL 309

Don't impose your wish in choosing career of your children. Discuss with them with open mind & guide them. But don't force them.

LIFE SKILL 310

Don't be proud of money & luxurious life. Be proud of your virtues as good character, integrity & Patriotism.

LIFE SKILL 311

If you want to perform at top level in sports, you need focus & killing instinct. There's cut throat fight at top level. Meditation & yoga do help in this endeavor!

LIFE SKILL 312

For a happy, harmonious family, do 3 works together. Worship together, Eat together & read together. All hands on mobile at home is spoiling healthy family life.

LIFE SKILL 313

Use suave, kind words. None can see inside. We are judged by our words.

LIFE SKILL 314

Shun ego, envy, lust & hate. This way, everyday you can be your better version.

LIFE SKILL 315

Care, specially ones who need it. It is the best way to show love & creates everlasting memories.

LIFE SKILL 316

Smile often. Laugh a lot. Dream highest, but keep feet firmly on the ground.

LIFE SKILL 317

Follow your mind, heart & soul in important matters. No harm in seeking advice of wise friends & elders.

LIFE SKILL 318

Don't worry, worries don't solve any problem. Rather aggravate problem, as worrying decreases efficiency.

LIFE SKILL 319

Try to have adequate, peaceful sleep. Listening music, specially divine, before sleeping helps a lot. Stop worrying about sleep. This only spoils sleep. Take dinner, light, at least 3 hours before going to bed

LIFE SKILL 320

Have patience, don't make haste in any matter. Each work happens at the right time, neither before, nor later.

LIFE SKILL 321

If your plan fails, don't get sad. God may be having a better plan for you. So, start afresh with renewed zeal

LIFE SKILL 322

Ultimately, how you treat people counts. Matters little, how much educated, talented or rich you are!!

LIFE SKILL 323

If you have to study for long hours, have a break after 45 minutes. Preferably have a little nap in between. Then better learning, retention & less exertion

LIFE SKILL 324

For creative writing, use short sentences. Use idioms, phrases, quotes. These are ornaments of impressive writing.

LIFE SKILL 325

For effective public speaking, start slow & pick up gradually. Use relevant quotes of eminent personalities. Involve gathering frequently.

LIFE SKILL 326

For keeping good health & immunity, walk fast 45 minutes daily, preferably in a park. Or if feasible, 15 minute jogging.

LIFE SKILL 327

For healthy longevity, never bother about age. Have positive outlook, love, laugh, play & mix up with children. Many like Fauja Singh have run marathon at age of 100+

LIFE SKILL 328

Focus more inside than outside! All most important are inside: Joy, Virtues, Soul & Supreme Soul!

LIFE SKILL 329

Eliminate hate, grudge, differences & grievance! Activate love, respect, trust, gratitude, balance & benevolence!

LIFE SKILL 330

Have Patience Tolerance & Acceptance! Are not so easy, Come steadily with perseverance!

LIFE SKILL 331

Don't burn in envy, grudge & hate. They burn inside as an acid. Burn like a lamp, to spread light & warmth.

LIFE SKILL 332

Love, serve or cooperate: but sans expectations! No expectation, no frustration! Excessive expectations lead to devastation!

LIFE SKILL 333

Seek beauty in God, nature & all His manifestations! With positive perception, beauty is in everything, everywhere! For a cynic beauty is nowhere!

LIFE SKILL 334

Sadly world is fragmenting to pieces. Propagate peace, live in peace, not in pieces.

LIFE SKILL 335

LIFE is struggle. With faith, struggle fortifies us. But steady struggle can make or break us. Break if lack of faith & hope. Make if lot of faith in self & God!

LIFE SKILL 336

Be bold, boldness makes us braver! Fear makes weaker! Bearing pain stoically makes tolerant! Acceptance enhances forbearance

LIFE SKILL 337

We all commit mistakes! These ought to be followed by Acceptance, Amendment & Apology.

LIFE SKILL 338

Transmute adversities to opportunities! Cowards fret & fume at adversities! Braves turn to opportunities!

LIFE SKILL 339

Opportunities open for the resilients who knock repeatedly at the door of success. For the lazy, even the open doors of success shut down!

LIFE SKILL 340

Do charity, generosity, with no formality, no vanity! Don't feel you are doing it! Feel God is doing through you!

LIFE SKÍLL 341

One lamp lights thousands of lamps, sans diminishing own light! Likewise Truth, Kindness create, activate so many virtues in us!

LIFE SKILL 342

Promise, but only which you can keep. Unfulfilled promise can make a friend foe & diminish your prestige.

LIFE SKILL 343

Be grateful to all your teachers, even after you achieve great heights. They do have a role in shaping your splendid career

LIFE SKILL 344

Make prudent & pragmatic choices. Only choice is in our hands. Consequences aren't under our full control.

LIFE SKILL 345

Enjoy every moment of life, as it comes. Life is short, time fleets fast & there is no replay .

LIFE SKILL 346

Remain calm & quiet, as only then you can think proper & take wise decisions. Wrong decisions will give wrong results & frustration!

LIFE SKILL 347

Forgive quickly for little fault. Forgive after apology for major fault. But never forgive a hardened criminal. This will spoil him further & lure others to indulge in crimes.

LIFE SKILL 348

Observe self & every person keenly. Each observation can be inspiration. Observe everything, every phenomena keenly. You can learn & enhance knowledge this way.

LIFE SKILL 349

Take constructive criticism in good light. It improves. Also criticise anyone politely, logically without offending.

LIFE SKILL 350

Don't leave your nation, family to seek career abroad. For a diligent & brilliant, no dearth of

opportunities in own country. But go abroad for touring, if you can afford. It's beneficial.

LIFE SKILL 351

Don't stop at failures. Start again with renewed zeal. JK Rowling's Harry Potter was successful after many failures. Edison invented filament for electric bulb after hundreds of failures. Examples are endless.

LIFE SKILL 352

Don't undermine anything: Everything, every phenomena has a purpose. Every person you come across is important. Don't neglect anyone.

LIFE SKILL 353

Happy occasions don't come frequently. Celebrate these. But invite only those who came to you uninvited at sad occasions.

LIFE SKILL 354

Don't make haste in making friendship or any relationship. It's not easy to understand anyone very soon. Develop relation or friendship slowly & wisely. Only then these can be long lasting.

LIFE SKILL 355

Stop over thinking. Reduce over sensitivity! These do no good, only damage self. You can't control everything. So let it happen & let it be!

LIFE SKILL 356

Dream big. But achieve big too. This needs prudent pragmatic choices, then planning, then resolute & relentless pursuit!

LIFE SKILL 357

Be like a boat that floats on water. Let the boat flow with water, but don't let water flow over boat. Then boat must sink.

LIFE SKILL 358

Don't hate anyone, specially who love you.

Don't cheat anyone, specially who trust you.

Don't forget any friend or relation, specially who helped you!

LIFE SKILL 359

Hope but don't expect.

Have faith, but not blindly: rather apply due logic.

Trust, but not blindly, rather wisely.

LIFE SKILL 360

Start day by touching feet of parents. Their blessings will work wonders. Start by hugging, feeding a cow. It is proven destressing. And start with a prayer. Hopefully all day will be better with no despair!